Congressional
Research
Service

Unemployment Insurance: Programs and Benefits

Julie M. Whittaker
Specialist in Income Security

Katelin P. Isaacs
Analyst in Income Security

November 20, 2013

Congressional Research Service

7-5700

www.crs.gov

RL33362

CRS Report for Congress ───────────────────────

Prepared for Members and Committees of Congress

Summary

Various benefits may be available to unemployed workers to provide income support. When eligible workers lose their jobs, the Unemployment Compensation (UC) program may provide up to 26 weeks of income support through the payment of regular UC benefits. Unemployment benefits may be extended for up to 47 weeks by the temporarily authorized Emergency Unemployment Compensation (EUC08) program. Unemployment benefits may be extended for up to a further 13 or 20 weeks by the permanent Extended Benefit (EB) program under certain state economic conditions.

Certain groups of workers who lose their jobs because of international competition may qualify for income support through Trade Adjustment Act (TAA) programs. Unemployed workers may be eligible to receive Disaster Unemployment Assistance (DUA) benefits if they are not eligible for regular UC and if their unemployment may be directly attributed to a declared major disaster. Former U.S. military servicemembers may be eligible for unemployment benefits through the unemployment compensation for ex-servicemembers (UCX) program. The Emergency Unemployment Compensation Act of 1991 (P.L. 102-164) provides that ex-servicemembers be treated the same as other unemployed workers with respect to benefit levels, the waiting period for benefits, and benefit duration.

On January 2, 2013, the President signed P.L. 112-240, the American Taxpayer Relief Act of 2012. P.L. 112-240 extended the authorization for the EUC08 program through the week ending on or before January 1, 2014, as well as altered the structure and availability of EUC08 benefits in states. P.L. 112-240 also extended the temporary 100% federal financing of EB and the option to allow states to use three-year lookback calculations in their EB triggers through December 31, 2013.

For an overview of expiring UI provisions and their consequences for UI benefit availability and financing, see CRS Report R41508, *Expiring Unemployment Insurance Provisions*, by Katelin P. Isaacs.

For an explanation of the impact of sequestration on unemployment insurance benefits, see CRS Report R43133, *The Impact of Sequestration on Unemployment Insurance Benefits: Frequently Asked Questions*, by Katelin P. Isaacs and Julie M. Whittaker.

Contents

Figures

Tables

Appendixes

Contacts

Introduction

A variety of benefits may be available to unemployed workers to provide them with income support during a spell of unemployment. The cornerstone of this income support is the joint federal-state Unemployment Compensation (UC) program, which may provide income support through the payment of UC benefits for up to a maximum of 26 weeks.[1] Other programs that may provide workers with income support are more specialized. They may target special groups of workers, be automatically triggered by certain economic conditions, be temporarily created by Congress with a set expiration date, or target typically ineligible workers through a disaster declaration.

UC benefits may be extended at the state level by the permanent Extended Benefit (EB) program if high unemployment exists within the state. Once regular unemployment benefits are exhausted, the EB program may provide up to an additional 13 or 20 weeks of benefits, depending on worker eligibility, state law, and economic conditions in the state. The EB program is funded 50% by the federal government and 50% by the states, although the 2009 stimulus package (P.L. 111-5, as amended) temporarily provides for 100% federal funding of the EB program.

A temporary unemployment insurance program, the Emergency Unemployment Compensation (EUC08) program, began in July 2008. The authorization for the EUC08 program expires the week ending on or before January 1, 2014. Therefore, the last day of EUC08 availability is December 28, 2013 (December 29, 2013, for New York). This was the eighth temporary program Congress has created to provide extended unemployment compensation during an economic slowdown.[2] The EUC08 benefit is 100% federally funded. State UC agencies administer the EUC08 benefit along with regular UC benefits. As of June 29, 2013, EUC08 benefits are no longer available in North Carolina. See **Appendix A** for diagrams of the current unemployment benefits available to workers as well as a detailed diagram of the expansions and contractions of the EUC08 benefit.

Former U.S. military servicemembers may be eligible for unemployment benefits through the unemployment compensation for ex-servicemembers (UCX) program. The Emergency Unemployment Compensation Act of 1991 (P.L. 102-164) provides that ex-servicemembers be treated the same as other unemployed workers with respect to benefit levels, the waiting period for benefits, and benefit duration. (Please see CRS Report RS22440, *Unemployment Compensation (Insurance) and Military Service*, by Julie M. Whittaker.)

If an unemployed worker is not eligible to receive UC benefits and the worker's unemployment may be directly attributed to a declared major disaster, a worker may be eligible to receive Disaster Unemployment Assistance (DUA) benefits under the Stafford Act. The federal disaster

---

[1] Currently, Arkansas provides up to 25 weeks; Michigan, Missouri, and South Carolina provide up to 20 weeks; and the maximum duration of UC in Florida, Georgia, and North Carolina is variable, based on the state unemployment rate. For more details on these states with less than 26 weeks of UC available, see CRS Report R41859, *Unemployment Insurance: Consequences of Changes in State Unemployment Compensation Laws*, by Katelin P. Isaacs. In addition, the maximum UC duration in Montana is 28 weeks and Massachusetts is 30 weeks. In conjunction with benefits from the Extended Benefit (EB) program, however, UC duration is capped at 26 weeks.

[2] The other temporary programs became effective in 1958, 1961, 1972, 1975, 1982, 1991, and 2002. For details on these programs, see CRS Report RL34340, *Extending Unemployment Compensation Benefits During Recessions*, by Julie M. Whittaker and Katelin P. Isaacs.

---

declaration will include information on whether DUA benefits are available. For information on Disaster Unemployment Assistance, see CRS Report RS22022, *Disaster Unemployment Assistance (DUA)*, by Julie M. Whittaker.

Certain groups of workers who lose their jobs because of international competition may qualify for additional or supplemental support through Trade Adjustment Act (TAA) programs or (for certain workers aged 50 or older) through Reemployment Trade Adjustment Assistance (RTAA). This report does not describe the TAA or RTAA programs. (Please see CRS Report R42012, *Trade Adjustment Assistance for Workers*, by Benjamin Collins for information on these programs.)

Within the unemployment insurance system, there are also two programs that provide alternative benefits in lieu of benefits through the UC program: the Short-Time Compensation (STC) or "work sharing" program and the Self-Employment Assistance (SEA) program. For details on STC, see CRS Report R40689, *Compensated Work Sharing Arrangements (Short-Time Compensation) as an Alternative to Layoffs*, by Julie M. Whittaker. For details on SEA, see CRS Report R41253, *The Self-Employment Assistance (SEA) Program*, by Katelin P. Isaacs.

Some, but not all, types of unemployment insurance expenditures are subject to sequestration under the Budget Control Act of 2011 (P.L. 112-25, as amended).[3] UC, UCX, and UCFE payments are exempt from the sequester, but EB, EUC08, and most forms of administrative funding are subject to the sequester reductions. For details on the impact of sequestration on UI benefits, see CRS Report R43133, *The Impact of Sequestration on Unemployment Insurance Benefits: Frequently Asked Questions*, by Katelin P. Isaacs and Julie M. Whittaker.

This report describes three kinds of unemployment benefits: regular UC, EB, and EUC08. The report explains their basic eligibility requirements, benefits, and financing structure.

Unemployment Compensation

UC is a joint federal-state program financed by federal taxes under the Federal Unemployment Tax Act (FUTA) and by state payroll taxes under the State Unemployment Tax Acts (SUTA). The UC program has a direct impact on almost every business in the United States as most businesses are subject to state and federal unemployment taxes. An estimated $5.3 billion in federal unemployment taxes and $50.5 billion in state unemployment taxes will be collected in FY2014. In FY2014, states will spend a projected $40.5 billion on regular UC benefits. Approximately 130.3 million jobs are covered by the UC program. At the end of the week of August 17, 2013, 2.9 million unemployed workers received UC. As of July 2013, the 12-month average weekly UC benefit was $307.

Originally, the intent of the UC program, among other things, was to help counter economic fluctuations such as recessions.[4] This intent is reflected in the current UC program's funding and benefit structure. When the economy grows, UC program revenue rises through increased tax

---

[3] For details on the sequester under the Budget Control Act of 2011, as amended, see CRS Report R42050, *Budget "Sequestration" and Selected Program Exemptions and Special Rules*, coordinated by Karen Spar.

[4] See, for example, President Franklin Roosevelt's remarks at the signing of the Social Security Act at http://www.ssa.gov/history/fdrstmts html#signing.

revenues while UC program spending falls as fewer workers are unemployed. The effect of collecting more taxes than are spent dampens demand in the economy. This also creates a surplus of funds or a "cushion" of available funds for the UC program to draw upon during a recession. In a recession, UC tax revenue falls and UC program spending rises as more workers lose their jobs and receive UC benefits. The increased amount of UC payments to unemployed workers dampens the economic effect of earnings losses by injecting additional funds into the economy.

Authorization

The underlying framework of the UC system is contained in the Social Security Act. Title III of the act authorizes grants to states for the administration of state UC laws, Title IX authorizes the various components of the federal Unemployment Trust Fund (UTF), and Title XII authorizes advances or loans to insolvent state UC programs.

Appropriation and Outlays

The federal government appropriates funds for federal and state UC program administration, the federal share of EB payments, the EUC08 program, and federal loans to insolvent state UC programs. In FY2013, states were projected to receive an estimated $4.7 billion from the federal government for the administration of their UC programs, $0.12 billion for the federal share of EB payments, and $25.7 billion for the temporary EUC08 program.[5]

Administration

The U.S. Department of Labor (DOL) administers the federal portion of the UC system, which operates in each state, the District of Columbia, Puerto Rico, and the Virgin Islands. Federal law sets broad rules that the 53 state programs must follow. These include the broad categories of workers that must be covered by the program, the method for triggering the EB and EUC08 programs, the floor on the highest state unemployment tax rate to be imposed on employers (5.4%), and how the states will repay UTF loans. If the states do not follow these rules, their employers may lose a portion of their state unemployment tax credit when their federal income tax is calculated. The federal tax pays for both federal and state administrative costs, the federal share of the EB program, loans to insolvent state UC accounts, and state employment services.[6]

Eligibility for Regular Unemployment Compensation

Broad Federal Guidelines Result in Different State Requirements

Whereas federal laws and regulations provide broad guidelines on UC benefit coverage, eligibility, and benefit determination, the specifics of regular UC benefits are determined by each state. This results in essentially 53 different programs. States determine UC benefit eligibility, payments, and duration through state laws and program regulations. Generally, UC eligibility is

---

[5] U.S. Department of Labor, *UI Outlook*, Midsession Review, July 2013, available at http://www.workforcesecurity.doleta.gov/unemploy/content/midsession_review.asp.

[6] For more information on job search assistance and job search training for unemployed workers, see CRS Report RL34251, *Federal Programs Available to Unemployed Workers*, coordinated by Katelin P. Isaacs.

based on attaining qualified wages and employment in covered work over a 12-month period (called a base period) prior to unemployment.

Base Period

The base period is the time period during which wages earned or hours/weeks worked are examined to determine a worker's monetary entitlement to UC. Almost all states use the first four of the last five completed calendar quarters preceding the filing of the claim as their base period. This may result in a lag of up to five months between the end of the base period and the date a worker becomes unemployed. As a result there are some instances when workers with substantial labor market attachment are ineligible for UC benefits. In particular, recent entrants to the workforce, or re-entrants, may be ineligible under this definition. Federal law allows states to develop expanded definitions of the base period.

A list of states' base periods can be found at http://ows.doleta.gov/unemploy/pdf/uilawcompar/ 2013/monetary.pdf in Table 3-2.

Alternative Base Period

Almost two-thirds of states allow the use of an alternative base period (ABP) for workers failing to qualify under the regular base period. For example, if the worker fails to qualify using wages and employment in the first four of the last five completed calendar quarters, then the state might use wages and employment in the last four completed calendar quarters.

Extended Base Period

Several states allow workers who have no wages in the current base period to use older wages and employment under certain conditions. These conditions typically involve illness or injury. For example, a worker who was injured on the job and who has collected workers' compensation benefits may use wages and employment preceding the date of the worker's injury to establish eligibility.

Base Period Provisions in the 2009 Stimulus Package

The 2009 stimulus package (P.L. 111-5) provided up to $7 billion to states as an incentive to make changes to their unemployment programs. States had to apply for these funds by August 22, 2011, and no payment could occur after September 30, 2011. A total of $4.4 billion of the $7 billion fund was distributed to states. By law, the remaining $2.6 billion became unrestricted funds within the Federal Unemployment Account of the Unemployment Trust Fund.

One-third of a state's share of this amount was contingent on state law allowing use of a base period that includes the most recently completed calendar quarter before the start of the benefit year for the purpose of determining UC eligibility. The remaining two-thirds of a state's share of the $7 billion was contingent on qualifying for the first one-third payment (by adopting an alternative base period definition), plus adopting two of four additional provisions.[7]

---

[7] For more information on unemployment modernization provisions in the American Recovery and Reinvestment Act (continued...)

Qualifying Wages or Employment

All states require a worker to have earned a certain amount of wages or to have worked for a certain period of time (or both) within the base period to be monetarily eligible to receive any UC benefits. The methods that states use to determine monetary eligibility vary greatly.

Multiple of High-Quarter Wages. Under this method, workers must earn a certain dollar amount in the quarter with the highest earnings of their base period. Workers must also earn total base-period wages that are a multiple—typically 1.5—of the high-quarter wages. For example, if a worker earns $5,000 in the high quarter, the worker must earn at least another $2,500 in the rest of the base period. States require earnings in more than one quarter to minimize the likelihood that workers with earnings in only one quarter receive benefits. Although the worker might be monetarily eligible based upon the earnings accrued in one quarter, these "multiple of high quarter wages" states do not deem those workers to be substantially attached to the labor market.

Multiple of Weekly Benefit Amount. Under this method, the state first computes the worker's weekly benefit amount. The worker must have earned a multiple—often 40—of this amount during the base period. For example, if a worker's weekly benefit amount equals $100, then the worker will need base period earnings of 40 times $100, or $4,000, before any UC would be paid. Most states also require wages in at least two quarters. Some states have weighted schedules that require varying multiples for varying weekly benefits. Some states allow a reduced weekly benefit amount to meet the multiple requirement.

Flat Qualifying Amount. States using this method require a certain dollar amount of total wages to be earned during the base period. This method is used by most states with an annual-wage requirement for determining the weekly benefit and by some states with a high-quarter wage/weekly benefit requirement.

Weeks/Hours of Employment. Under this method, the worker must have worked a certain number of weeks/hours at a certain weekly/hourly wage.

Data Collection Considerations

The wide variation seen in state UC program laws and regulations also exists among the states' data collections. All states collect information on earnings by quarter for each worker. A handful of states collect information on the number of weeks worked during the base period. Even fewer states collect information on the numbers of hours worked during a quarter. As a result, most states use information on quarters worked, quarterly earnings, and cumulative earnings in determining eligibility and the amount of benefit.[8] It does not appear that any state uses both hours of work and weeks of work in the base period calculation.

(...continued)

of 2009 (P.L. 111-5), please see CRS Report R40368, *Unemployment Insurance Provisions in the American Recovery and Reinvestment Act of 2009*, by Julie M. Whittaker.

[8] The U.S. DOL *2013 Comparison of State Unemployment Insurance Laws* reports that the following states used the measure of "weeks" in determination of eligibility or benefit amount: New Jersey, Ohio, and Pennsylvania. Only Washington appears to use the number of hours worked in eligibility or benefit determination.

Determination and Duration of Regular Unemployment Compensation

Generally, benefits are based on wages for covered work over a 12-month period (the "base period" or "alternative base period," described above). Most state benefit formulas replace half of a claimant's average weekly wage up to a weekly maximum. All states disregard some earnings during unemployment as an incentive to take short-term or part-time work while searching for a permanent position. Generally, the worker's UC payment equals the difference between the weekly benefit amount and earnings.

Table 1 lists the minimum and maximum UC benefits for each state. Weekly maximums in July 2013 ranged from $133 (Puerto Rico) to $674 (Massachusetts) and, in states that provide dependents' allowances, up to $1,011 (Massachusetts). In July 2013, the average weekly benefit was $307. Benefits are available for up to 26 weeks in most states (30 weeks in Massachusetts; 28 weeks in Montana; 25 weeks in Arkansas; 20 weeks in Michigan, Missouri, and South Carolina; 12-23 weeks in Florida, depending on the state unemployment rate; 14-20 weeks in Georgia, depending on the state unemployment rate; and 12-20 weeks in North Carolina, depending on the state unemployment rate).[9] Among individuals receiving benefits, the average regular UC benefit duration in July 2013 was 16.8 weeks. In July 2013, approximately 3 million unemployed workers received regular state UC benefits in a given week.

Table 1. State Unemployment Compensation Benefit Amounts, July 2013

(in dollars)

	Minimum Weekly UC Benefit Amount	Minimum If Dependents' Allowance[a]	Maximum Weekly UC Benefit Amount[b]	Maximum If Dependents' Allowance[a]
Alabama	45		265	
Alaska	56	128	370	442
Arizona	122		240	
Arkansas	81		451	
California	40		450	
Colorado	25		529	
Connecticut	15	30	591	666
Delaware	20		330	
District of Columbia	50		359	
Florida	32		275	
Georgia	44		330	
Hawaii	5		534	
Idaho	72		357	
Illinois	51	77	413	562

---

[9] For more details on states with reduced maximum durations in their UC programs, see CRS Report R41859, *Unemployment Insurance: Consequences of Changes in State Unemployment Compensation Laws*, by Katelin P. Isaacs.

	Minimum Weekly UC Benefit Amount	Minimum If Dependents' Allowance[a]	Maximum Weekly UC Benefit Amount[b]	Maximum If Dependents' Allowance[a]
Indiana	37		390	
Iowa	60	73	408	501
Kansas	117		469	
Kentucky	39		415	
Louisiana	10		247	
Maine	66	99	378	567
Maryland	50	90	430	
Massachusetts	33	49	674	1,011
Michigan	117	147	362	
Minnesota	24		393	610
Mississippi	30		235	
Missouri	35		320	
Montana	132		464	
Nebraska	70		362	
Nevada	16		407	
New Hampshire	32		427	
New Jersey	87	100	624	
New Mexico	76	114	407	457
New York	64		405	
North Carolina	15		350	
North Dakota	43		570	
Ohio	115		413	557
Oklahoma	16		386	
Oregon	126		538	
Pennsylvania	70	78	573	581
Puerto Rico	7		133	
Rhode Island	42	92	566	707
South Carolina	42		326	
South Dakota	28		345	
Tennessee	30	80	275	325
Texas	62		440	
Utah	26		479	
Vermont	58		425	
Virginia	54		378	
Virgin Islands	33		491	
Washington	148		624	
West Virginia	24		424	

	Minimum Weekly UC Benefit Amount	Minimum If Dependents' Allowance[a]	Maximum Weekly UC Benefit Amount[b]	Maximum If Dependents' Allowance[a]
Wisconsin	54		363	
Wyoming	34		471	

Source: Congressional Research Service (CRS) table compiled from *Significant Provisions of State Unemployment Insurance Laws, July 2013*, U.S. Department of Labor, Employment and Training Administration, at http://www.workforcesecurity.doleta.gov/unemploy/content/sigpros/2010-2019/July2013.pdf.

a. The figures for minimum and maximum benefits include dependents' allowances for the maximum number of dependents.

b. If a state has dependents' allowances and only one amount is given, the maximum is the same with or without the allowance.

UC Benefit Financing: Unemployment Taxes on Employers

UC benefits are financed through employer taxes.[10] The federal taxes on employers are under the authority of the Federal Unemployment Tax Act (FUTA), and the state taxes are under the authority given by the State Unemployment Tax Acts (SUTA). These taxes are deposited in the appropriate accounts within the Unemployment Trust Fund (UTF).

Federal Unemployment Tax Act

The net FUTA tax rate on employers in states with UC programs that are in compliance with all federal rules is 0.6% on the first $7,000 of each worker's earnings per year. The FUTA tax rate for employers is 6.0% on the first $7,000 of each worker's earnings, but a 5.4% credit against the federal FUTA tax is available to employers in states with complying UC programs, bringing the net FUTA tax down to 0.6%.[11] The 0.6% FUTA tax funds both federal and state administrative costs as well as the federal share of the EB program, loans to insolvent state UC accounts, and state employment services. Federal law defines which jobs a state UC program must cover, provides rules concerning state borrowing from the UTF, and provides broad guidelines concerning benefit eligibility, in order for the state's employers to avoid paying the maximum FUTA tax rate (6.0%) on the first $7,000 of each employee's annual pay. The U.S. DOL projects that $5.3 billion in FUTA taxes were collected in FY2013.

Federal law requires that a state must cover jobs in firms that pay at least $1,500 in wages during any calendar quarter or employ at least one worker in each of 20 weeks in the current or prior year. The FUTA tax is not paid by government or nonprofit employers, but state programs must cover government workers and all workers in nonprofits that employ at least four workers in each of 20 weeks in the current or prior year.[12]

---

[10] For a more detailed description of UC financing, see CRS Report RS22077, *Unemployment Compensation (UC) and the Unemployment Trust Fund (UTF): Funding UC Benefits*, by Julie M. Whittaker.

[11] In tax year 2013, 13 states and the Virgin Islands had a state tax credit reduction applied to the calculation of the FUTA tax. This tax credit reduction ranged from 0.6%-1.2%. For more details, see CRS Report RS22954, *The Unemployment Trust Fund (UTF): State Insolvency and Federal Loans to States*, by Julie M. Whittaker.

[12] Employers who are required to provide unemployment insurance coverage, but who are not required to pay the FUTA tax, generally reimburse state governments for the benefit payments related to their workers. States are reimbursed for expenditures related to federal workers by the federal government.

Congress first passed a temporary FUTA surtax in 1976 and since 1983 the surtax had been applied as 0.2% on the first $7,000 of employee wages for a net total FUTA tax rate of 0.8%. P.L. 111-92 was the last law to extend the authorization of the FUTA surtax (through June 2011). Since July 1, 2011, the authorization of the 0.2% FUTA surtax has lapsed.

ARRA Temporary Changes to Federal Financing of Unemployment Benefits

ARRA (P.L. 111-5) made several important, albeit temporary, changes to the federal role in financing unemployment benefit programs. Under ARRA (as amended), the federal government temporarily uses UTF monies to finance 100% of EB payments through December 31, 2013 (under permanent law EB payments are financed 50% by the federal government and 50% by states). The federal government also used UTF funds to finance a $500 million transfer to states for administering unemployment programs, and used UTF funds for the $7 billion in incentive monies to states for undertaking modernization of their unemployment programs. ARRA also changed the financing of the EUC08 program, which from its implementation in July 2008 had been financed from the UTF, but starting with enactment of ARRA (on February 17, 2009) has been financed from general revenues of the Treasury. States continue to finance regular UC through SUTA revenues.[13]

State Unemployment Tax Acts

States levy their own payroll taxes (SUTA taxes) on employers to fund regular UC benefits and the state share of the EB program. The state unemployment tax rate on an employer is "experience rated" in all states, that is, the SUTA rate is based on the amount of UC paid to former employees. Generally, the more UC benefits paid to its former employees, the higher the tax rate of the employer, up to a maximum established by state law. The experience rating is intended to ensure an equitable distribution of UC program taxes among employers in relationship to their use of the UC program, and to encourage a stable workforce. State ceilings on taxable wages in July 2013 ranged from the $7,000 FUTA federal ceiling (three states) to $39,800 (Washington State). The minimum SUTA rates ranged from 0.00% (five states) to 2.80% (Pennsylvania) in July 2013. Maximum SUTA rates ranged from 5.4% (nine states) to 12.27% (Massachusetts) in July 2013. A projected $50.5 billion in SUTA taxes will be collected in FY2014.

State UC revenue is deposited in the U.S. Treasury. These deposits are counted as federal revenue in the budget. State accounts within the UTF are credited for this revenue. The U.S. Treasury reimburses states from the appropriate UTF state accounts for their benefit payments. These payments do not require an annual appropriation, but the reimbursements do count as federal budget outlays.

---

[13] For details on changes to UI programs under ARRA (P.L. 111-5) beyond these financing provisions, see CRS Report R40368, *Unemployment Insurance Provisions in the American Recovery and Reinvestment Act of 2009*, by Julie M. Whittaker.

Table 2. State Unemployment Taxes: Taxable Wage Base and Rates, July 2013

State	2013 Wages Subject to Tax ($)	2013 Minimum State Unemployment Tax (%)[a]	2013 Maximum State Unemployment Tax (%)[a]
Alabama	8,000	0.59	6.74
Alaska	36,900	1.54	5.40
Arizona	7,000	0.02	6.67
Arkansas	12,000	0.10	6.00
California	7,000	1.50	6.20
Colorado	11,300	0.66	8.90
Connecticut	15,000	1.90	6.80
Delaware	10,500	0.10	8.00
DC	9,000	1.60	7.00
Florida	8,000	1.02	5.40
Georgia	9,500	0.02	5.40
Hawaii	39,600	1.80	6.40
Idaho	34,800	0.78	6.80
Illinois	12,900	0.55	8.95
Indiana	9,500	0.53	7.90
Iowa	26,000	0.00	8.50
Kansas	8,000	0.11	9.40
Kentucky	9,300	1.00	10.00
Louisiana	7,700	0.10	6.20
Maine	12,000	0.89	8.21
Maryland	8,500	1.00	10.50
Massachusetts	14,000	1.26	12.27
Michigan	9,500	0.06	10.30
Minnesota	29,000	0.67	10.81
Mississippi	14,000	0.45	5.40
Missouri	13,000	0.00	9.75
Montana	27,900	0.62	6.12
Nebraska	9,000	0.00	5.40
Nevada	26,900	0.25	5.40
New Hampshire	14,000	2.60	7.00
New Jersey	30,900	1.20	7.00
New Mexico	22,900	0.10	5.40
New York	8,500	0.90	8.90
North Carolina	20,900	0.00	6.84
North Dakota	31,800	0.17	9.78

State	2013 Wages Subject to Tax ($)	2013 Minimum State Unemployment Tax (%)[a]	2013 Maximum State Unemployment Tax (%)[a]
Ohio	9,000	0.30	8.40
Oklahoma	20,100	0.30	9.20
Oregon	34,100	2.20	5.40
Pennsylvania	8,500	2.80	10.89
Puerto Rico	7,000	2.40	5.40
Rhode Island	20,200[b]	1.69	9.79
South Carolina	12,000	0.09	7.85
South Dakota	13,000	0.00	9.50
Tennessee	9,000	0.40	10.00
Texas	9,000	0.54	7.35
Utah	30,300	0.40	7.40
Vermont	16,000	1.30	8.40
Virginia	8,000	0.68	6.78
Virgin Islands	23,600	1.50	6.00
Washington	39,800	0.17	5.84
West Virginia	12,000	1.50	7.50
Wisconsin	14,000	0.27	9.80
Wyoming	23,800	0.63	10.00

Source: CRS table compiled from *Significant Provisions of State Unemployment Insurance Laws, July 2013*, U.S. Department of Labor, Employment and Training Administration, at http://www.workforcesecurity.doleta.gov/ unemploy/content/sigpros/2010-2019/July2013.pdf.

a. Tax rates apply only to experience-rated employers; states apply different rates to new employers. These rates reflect tax year 2013.

b. Or $21,700 for high tax group employers.

Generally, during economic expansions, FUTA and SUTA revenue collections will exceed UC outlays. During economic recessions, revenues generally will be less than UC outlays. For example, UTF outlays significantly exceeded trust fund revenue in FY2001-FY2004, and again starting in FY2008. From FY2005 to FY2007, UC revenue exceeded total UC outlays. **Table 3** lists the total revenue and outlays associated with the UC program from FY2001 through FY2013 (estimated).

Table 3. Revenue and Expenditures Associated with Unemployment Compensation, FY2001-FY2013

(in billions of dollars)

	2001	2002	2003	2004	2005	2006	2007	2008	2009	2010	2011	2012	2013a
UC revenue, total	**27.8**	**27.5**	**33.2**	**39.3**	**41.8**	**43.0**	**41.0**	**39.4**	**37.8**	**44.7**	**55.9**	**64.7**	**56.0**
Federal Unemployment Tax (FUTA)	6.9	6.6	6.5	6.6	6.7	7.1	7.3	7.2	6.7	6.4	6.6	5.4	5.3
State Unemployment Taxes (SUTA)	20.8	20.9	26.7	32.7	35.1	35.9	33.7	32.2	31.1	38.3	49.3	59.3	50.7
UC outlays, total	**28.1**	**50.9**	**54.3**	**42.5**	**32.6**	**31.5**	**32.7**	**43.0**	**119.7**	**156.3**	**116.8**	**90.4**	**68.0**
Regular benefits (UC)	27.3	42.0	42.0	36.9	31.2	30.2	31.4	38.1	75.3	63.0	48.5	44.3	40.9
Extended benefits (EB)	b	0.16	0.32	0.16	b	0.02	0.02	0.02	4.1	8.0	11.9	4.9	0.12
Emergency Unemployment Compensation (EUC08)	—	7.9	11	4.1	—	—	—	3.6	32.7	72.1	52.7	39.6	25.7
Federal Additional Compensation (FAC)	—	—	—	—	—	—	—	—	6.5	11.7	1.9	0.0	0.0
UCFE/UCXc	0.5	0.5	0.6	0.8	0.8	0.8	0.7	0.7	1.0	1.3	1.6	1.4	1.1
Trade Benefits	0.3	0.3	0.4	0.5	0.6	0.5	0.6	0.6	0.1	0.2	0.2	0.2	0.2
Administrative costs	**3.6**	**3.7**	**4.1**	**3.9**	**3.8**	**3.9**	**3.7**	**3.9**	**4.3**	**5.5**	**5.0**	**4.9**	**4.7**

Source: U.S. Department of Labor, *UI Outlook*, January 2001-July 2013, and updates.

a. Estimated for FY2013.

b. Less than $5 million.

c. UC benefits for federal employees (UCFE) and former military servicemembers (UCX).

Outstanding Loans from the Federal Unemployment Account

If a state trust fund account becomes insolvent, a state may borrow federal funds.[14] DOL maintains a list of all states with loans and includes the loan amounts.[15] States are charged interest on loans that are not repaid by the end of the fiscal year in which they were obtained.

The American Recovery and Reinvestment Act of 2009 (P.L. 111-5, the 2009 stimulus package) temporarily waived interest payments, and no interest accrued on interest payments that came due from the time the stimulus package was enacted (February 17, 2009) until December 31, 2010. Although states did pay interest during this period, they were still required to repay the principal on the underlying loans according to the schedule provided in federal law. If a state does not pay back loaned funds within the prescribed amount of time or make good progress as determined by the U.S. Secretary of Labor, the state unemployment tax credit will be reduced.

---

[14] For detailed information on loans to the states within the UTF, see CRS Report RS22954, *The Unemployment Trust Fund (UTF): State Insolvency and Federal Loans to States*, by Julie M. Whittaker.

[15] See http://www.workforcesecurity.doleta.gov/unemploy/budget.asp#tfloans.

Federal Additional Compensation

P.L. 111-5 created the now-expired Federal Additional Compensation (FAC), a $25 weekly benefit supplement for individuals receiving benefits from all unemployment compensation programs: UC, EUC08, EB, Disaster Unemployment Assistance (DUA), and Trade Adjustment Assistance (TAA). The authorization for the FAC $25 weekly benefit expired on May 29, 2010. It has not been extended by subsequent unemployment insurance legislation (P.L. 111-205; P.L. 111-312; P.L. 112-78; or P.L. 112-96).

If an unemployed individual was receiving any type of unemployment benefit—UC, EUC08, EB, DUA, or TAA—from February 22, 2009 (February 23, 2009, for New York) until May 29, 2010 (May 30, 2010, for New York), that individual continued to receive the weekly FAC until he or she exhausted all unemployment benefits from all unemployment programs (i.e., UC, EUC08, EB, DUA, and TAA) or until December 11, 2010 (December 12, 2010, for New York), whichever date came first. Individuals who began receiving unemployment benefits after May 29, 2010 (May 30, 2010, for New York) did not receive the FAC. All FAC payments have ended.

Emergency Unemployment Compensation Program[16]

On June 30, 2008, the President signed the Supplemental Appropriations Act of 2008 (P.L. 110-252) into law. Title IV of this act created a new temporary unemployment insurance program, the EUC08 program. This is the eighth time Congress created a federal temporary program that extended unemployment compensation during an economic slowdown. Until February 16, 2009, the EUC08 program was financed with funds within the UTF. However, with the passage of P.L. 111-5, the EUC08 benefit is now 100% federally funded from general funds within the U.S. Treasury. State UC agencies administer the EUC08 benefit along with regular UC benefits.

Congress has amended the EUC08 program 11 times. Some of these laws have changed the structure and availability of EUC08 benefits. Mostly recently, P.L. 112-240, the American Taxpayer Relief Act of 2012, authorized EUC08 benefits until the week ending on or before January 1, 2014. Thus, the EUC08 program is authorized in all states until December 28, 2013 (December 29, 2013, for New York).

See **Appendix B** for a summary of public laws, benefits, effective dates, and financing issues related to the EUC08 program.

Previous Temporary Unemployment Compensation Extensions

Previously, Congress acted seven times—in 1958, 1961, 1971, 1974, 1982, 1991, and 2002—to establish similar temporary programs of extended UC benefits. These programs extended the period an individual might claim UC benefits (ranging from an additional 6 to 33 weeks) and had

---

[16] For an expanded version of this section, see CRS Report R42444, *Emergency Unemployment Compensation (EUC08): Current Status of Benefits*, by Julie M. Whittaker and Katelin P. Isaacs.

expiration dates.[17] Some extensions took into account state economic conditions; many temporary programs considered the state's total unemployment rate (TUR) or the state's insured unemployment rate (IUR) or both.

EUC08 Benefit Amounts, Tiers, and Duration

The amount of the EUC08 benefit is the equivalent of the eligible individual's weekly regular UC benefit and includes any applicable dependents' allowances. Since the creation of the EUC08 program in June 2008, Congress has made several changes to the structure of the EUC08 program. These structural changes have consequences for the availability of EUC08 tiers and benefits in states.

See **Figure A-1** for the flow of available unemployment insurance benefits—including EUC08 (plus, UC and EB).[18]

EUC08 benefits are no longer available in North Carolina due to enactment of a state law that violated the "nonreduction" rule.[19]

Current EUC08 Benefit Availability

The EUC08 program has been amended 11 times, most recently by P.L. 112-240.[20] The EUC08 benefit amount is equal to the eligible individual's weekly regular UC benefits and includes any applicable dependents' allowances. The most recent modifications to the underlying structure of the EUC08 program were made by P.L. 112-96. These modifications included changes to the number of weeks available in each EUC08 tier as well as the state unemployment rates required to have an active tier in that state. These requirements were implemented during 2012 in three separate phases.[21] Currently the following weeks of benefits are available in the tiers listed below: See **Figure A-2** for a diagram of EUC08 benefits available from 2008 to the present.

- **Tier I** is available in all states, except North Carolina, with up to 14 weeks of EUC08 benefits provided to eligible individuals.

---

[17] For more information on these programs, see CRS Report RL34340, *Extending Unemployment Compensation Benefits During Recessions*, by Julie M. Whittaker and Katelin P. Isaacs.

[18] Calendar dates provided in this section refer to all states except New York. New York defines a benefit week differently than all other states. In New York, a benefit week is a period from Monday through Sunday rather than Sunday through Saturday, as in all other states. Therefore, all effective dates for New York are one day later than the dates listed.

[19] North Carolina enacted legislation in February 2013 that included a provision to actively reduce UC weekly benefit amounts in the state. Effective on or after July 1, 2013, this state law provision violated the "nonreduction" rule and, therefore, terminated the EUC08 agreement between North Carolina and the Secretary of the U.S. Department of Labor. For more information on the "nonreduction" rule of EUC08, see CRS Report R41859, *Unemployment Insurance: Consequences of Changes in State Unemployment Compensation Laws*, by Katelin P. Isaacs.

[20] The 11 amendments are P.L. 110-449, P.L. 111-5, P.L. 111-92, P.L. 111-118, P.L. 111-144, P.L. 111-157, P.L. 111-205, P.L. 111-312, P.L. 112-78, P.L. 112-96, and P.L. 112-240. Summary details on all of these laws are provided in Table 1 of CRS Report R42444, *Emergency Unemployment Compensation (EUC08): Current Status of Benefits*, by Julie M. Whittaker and Katelin P. Isaacs.

[21] See CRS Report R42444, *Emergency Unemployment Compensation (EUC08): Current Status of Benefits*, by Julie M. Whittaker and Katelin P. Isaacs for details on how these changes were implemented.

- **Tier II** is available if the state's total unemployment rate (TUR)[22] is at least 6%, with up to 14 weeks provided to eligible individuals in those states (not available in North Carolina).

- **Tier III** is available if the state's TUR is at least 7% (or an insured unemployment rate, IUR,[23] of at least 4%), with up to 9 weeks of provided to eligible individuals in those states (not available in North Carolina).

- **Tier IV** is if the state's TUR is at least 9% or the IUR is 5%, with up to 10 weeks provided to eligible individuals in those states (not available in North Carolina).

Current EUC08 Program Expiration

All tiers of EUC08 benefits are temporary and expire in the week ending on or before January 1, 2014. Thus, on December 28, 2013 (December 29, 2013, for New York), the EUC08 program ends. There is no "grandfathering" of any EUC08 benefit after that date.

Additional Eligibility Requirements for EUC08

First Claimed Regular UC Benefits On or After May 7, 2006

Applicants must have been eligible for regular UC benefits and have exhausted their rights to regular UC compensation with respect to a benefit year that expired during or after the week of May 6, 2007.[24] For most states, this would apply to individuals who had filed UC claims with an effective date of May 7, 2006, or later. For the state of New York this would apply to original claims filed with an effective date of May 1, 2006, or later.[25]

Exhausted Regular UC Benefit

The right to regular UC benefits for an individual must be exhausted to be eligible for EUC08 benefits. Although federal laws and regulations provide broad guidelines on regular UC benefit coverage and eligibility determination, the specifics of regular UC benefits are determined by

---

[22] The TUR is the ratio of unemployed workers to all workers (employed and unemployed) in the labor market. The TUR is essentially a weekly version of the unemployment rate published by the Bureau of Labor Statistics (BLS) and based on data from the BLS' monthly Current Population Survey.

[23] The IUR is the ratio of UC claimants divided by individuals in UC-covered jobs. The IUR is substantially different from the TUR because it excludes several important groups: self-employed workers, unpaid family workers, workers in certain not-for-profit organizations, and several other, primarily seasonal, categories of workers. In addition to those unemployed workers whose last jobs were in the excluded employment, the insured unemployed rate excludes the following: those who have exhausted their UC benefits (even if they receive EB or EUC08 benefits); new entrants or reentrants to the labor force; disqualified workers whose unemployment is considered to have resulted from their own actions rather than from economic conditions; and eligible unemployed persons who do not file for benefits.

[24] Arkansas has a unique approach to calculating a benefit year. In Arkansas, the benefit year begins the first day of the quarter in which an individual files a valid UC claim. Thus, it is unlikely that many individuals in Arkansas who filed UC claims before July 2006 would be eligible to receive EUC08 benefits.

[25] Note that the effective date is not necessarily the actual date when an individual filed for UC. A claim filed on May 10, 2006, may have had an earlier effective date if a state allows retroactive claims.

---

each state. As noted earlier, this results in 53 different programs.[26] In particular, states determine UC benefit eligibility, amount, and duration through state laws and program regulations.[27]

"20 Weeks" of Full-Time Insured Employment or Equivalent

In addition to all state requirements for regular UC eligibility, the EUC08 program requires claimants to have at least 20 weeks of full-time insured employment or the equivalent in insured wages in their base period. The definition of "20 weeks" is discussed in the "Methods for Determining 20 Weeks of Full-Time Insured Employment" section of this report.

Reemployment and Eligibility Assessments (REAs)

P.L. 112-96 amended EUC08 law to require states to provide reemployment and eligibility assessments to most EUC08 claimants. EUC08 claimants must participate in reemployment services if referred. States receive $85 in federal funding per EUC08 claimant who receives reemployment and eligibility assessments.

EUC08 Financing

Until February 16, 2009, the EUC08 program was federally financed from the extended unemployment compensation account (EUCA) within the Unemployment Trust Fund (UTF). With the passage of the 2009 stimulus package (P.L. 111-5), however, EUC08 is now financed from general funds of the U.S. Treasury through the expiration of the EUC08 program. States do not need to repay these funds.

Interaction of EUC08 Benefits and Qualifying for a "Second Benefit Year"

The relationships between the various unemployment compensation programs currently available—regular UC, EUC08, and EB—have meant that unemployed workers who participate in additional paid work (while receiving benefits or temporarily stopping benefits) may create a new entitlement to regular UC as part of a "second benefit year." This new entitlement may be based on significantly lower earnings and/or fewer hours of employment, which could then lower an individual's weekly unemployment benefits.

This situation exists because (1) the EUC08 and EB laws require individuals to exhaust all regular UC benefits prior to being eligible to receive EUC08 or EB benefits and (2) after 52 weeks (i.e., after an individual's first benefit year) states are required to begin checking for any additional work performed by beneficiaries that would make them eligible for additional state UC benefits before any additional EUC08 or EB benefits would be paid.

---

[26] The 50 states, the District of Columbia, Puerto Rico, and the Virgin Islands provide UC benefits to their workers.

[27] Individuals in the Massachusetts and Montana UC programs may have regular UC durations that exceed 26 weeks. Those additional weeks are considered to be "sharable" compensation if the state is in an active EB period and these weeks are paid as if they were EB payments during those periods. The additional weeks of regular UC beyond 26 are not used to calculate EUC08 duration.

Because some eligible individuals in many states may have been entitled to more than 52 weeks of UI benefits, states are required by federal law to identify individuals who established a new entitlement to regular UC benefits via additional qualifying employment (even if the work was part-time, seasonal, or low-pay and did not result in permanent employment). This potential new entitlement means that states must shift back eligible individuals to regular UC (beginning a second benefit year) from EUC08 and EB. The amount of the new regular UC benefits may be significantly lower than the individual's (first benefit year) EUC08 and EB benefits.

P.L. 111-205 addressed this "second year benefit" issue for the EUC08 program. It did not address the equivalent issue in the EB program. Effective July 22, 2010, individuals who currently receive EUC08 or EB benefits, but have been determined by states to be eligible for a second benefit year based on additional work are allowed to opt to continue in the EUC08 program if their weekly unemployment benefits would be reduced by at least $100 or 25% by switching back to the regular UC program based on their additional employment. Only beneficiaries who are determined by their state to have a second benefit year after the date of enactment are allowed this option. Those beneficiaries who were determined by their state prior to July 22, 2010, to have a second benefit year entitlement do not have this option.

EUC08 and EB Interactions

The EUC08 program should not be confused with the similarly named EB program (see description below). The EUC08 program is temporary and the availability of each EUC08 tier depends on state unemployment rate and calendar date. The EB program is permanently authorized and applies only to certain states on the basis of state unemployment conditions specified in law.

Prior to the enactment of P.L. 112-96, states were permitted to determine which benefit, EB or EUC08, was paid first. Alaska was the only state to pay EB first when this option was available.

P.L. 112-96 now requires that states pay EUC08 benefits before EB benefits.

The activation or deactivation of a particular tier of EUC08 follows the same rules as found in the EB program. See the section titled "How an Extended Benefit Period Is Activated (and Deactivated)" for details.

Extended Benefit Program

The EB program was established by the Federal-State Extended Unemployment Compensation Act of 1970 (EUCA), P.L. 91-373 (26 U.S.C. 3304, note). EUCA may extend receipt of unemployment benefits (extended benefits) at the state level if certain economic situations exist within the state.

The EB program is triggered when a state's IUR or TUR reaches certain levels. All states must pay up to 13 weeks of EB if the IUR for the previous 13 weeks is at least 5% and is 120% of the average of the rates for the same 13-week period in each of the two previous years. There are two other optional thresholds that states may choose. (States may choose one, two, or none.) If the state has chosen a given option, they would provide the following:

- Option 1: an additional 13 weeks of benefits if the state's IUR is at least 6%, regardless of previous years' averages.

- Option 2: an additional 13 weeks of benefits if the state's TUR is at least 6.5% and is at least 110% of the state's average TUR for the same 13 weeks in either of the previous two years; an additional 20 weeks of benefits if the TUR is at least 8% and is at least 110% of the state's average TUR for the same 13 weeks in either of the previous two years.

Each state's IUR and TUR are determined by the state of residence (agent state) of the unemployed worker rather than by the state of employment (liable state). EB benefits are not "grandfathered" when a state triggers "off" the program. When a state triggers "off" of an EB period, all EB benefit payments in the state cease immediately regardless of individual entitlement.[28]

Temporary EB Trigger Modifications in P.L. 111-312

P.L. 111-312 made some technical changes to certain triggers in the EB program. P.L. 111-312, as amended, allows states to temporarily use lookback calculations based on three years of unemployment rate data (rather than the permanent-law lookback of two years of data) as part of their mandatory IUR and optional TUR triggers if states would otherwise trigger off or not be on a period of EB benefits. Using a two-year vs. a three-year EB trigger lookback is an important adjustment because some states are likely to trigger off of their EB periods in the near future despite high, sustained—but not increasing—unemployment rates.

States implement the lookback changes individually by amending their state UC laws. These state law changes must be written in such a way that if the two-year lookback is working and the state would have an active EB program, no action would be taken. But if a two-year lookback is not working as part of an EB trigger and the state is not triggered on to an EB period, then the state would be able to use a three-year lookback. This temporary option to use three-year EB trigger lookbacks expires the week on or before December 31, 2013.

How an Extended Benefit Period Is Activated (and Deactivated)

The timing of when an EB period is activated depends on whether the trigger is based on the state's IUR or TUR.

- If EB is activated based upon the IUR (triggers "on"), the EB period is immediately in effect. Few states trigger on to EB using an IUR based measure.

- If EB is activated based upon the TUR, the activation is subject to a different requirement. By law, a state triggering on to an EB period based upon a TUR based trigger will begin to offer those benefits on the third week after the first week for which there is a state "on" indicator.[29]

The analogous rules apply for deactivating an EB period.

---

[28] EB benefits on interstate claims are limited to two extra weeks unless both the agent state (e.g., Texas) and liable state (e.g., Louisiana) are in an EB period.

[29] Section 203(a)(1) of P.L. 91-373, as amended.

- If an EB period is deactivated based upon the state failing to meet IUR based trigger requirements (triggers "off"), the EB period is immediately ended.

- If an EB period triggers off based upon a state failing to meet TUR based trigger requirements, the EB period will end on the third week after the first week for which there is a state "off" indicator.[30]

Special Rule

By federal law, no EB period shall last for a period of less than 13 consecutive weeks, and no EB period may begin before the 14th week after the close of a prior EB period with respect to such state.[31]

The Department of Labor produces trigger notices indicating which states qualify for both EB and EUC08 benefits and provides the beginning and ending dates of payable periods for each qualifying state. The trigger notices covering state eligibility for these programs can be found at http://ows.doleta.gov/unemploy/claims_arch.asp. The IUR statistics change weekly, as they are based upon weekly programmatic data. The TUR statistics change monthly, as they are based upon monthly Local Area Unemployment Statistics (LAUS) data.[32]

Additional Eligibility Requirements for EB

The EB program imposes additional federal restrictions on individual eligibility for benefits beyond the state requirements for regular UC. The EB program requires that a worker make a "systematic and sustained" work search. Furthermore, the worker may not receive benefits if he or she refused an offer of "suitable" work, which is defined as "any work within such individual's capabilities." In addition, P.L. 97-35, among other items, amended the EUCA to require that claimants work at least 20 weeks of full-time insured employment or equivalent in insured wages during their base period.

The 2009 stimulus package affects a further requirement for EB eligibility. As the EB program has operated in the past, a beneficiary had to be *within* his or her original "benefit year"[33] when the EB program triggered "on" in their state in order to receive EB benefits. Thus, on the condition that the state triggered "on" during an individual's benefit year, he or she could receive EB benefits during the benefit year, or even after the benefit year expired, that is, at the time he or she exhausted regular unemployment compensation or EUC08 benefits even if this occurred after the expiration of the benefit year. However, if the state's most recent EB period triggered on *after* the individual's benefit year ended, the beneficiary would not receive EB. As a result, in states that have recently triggered "on" to EB because of rising unemployment rates, many individuals may be ineligible for EB benefits. For example, if an individual's benefit year expired in July 2008, this person would be ineligible for EB benefits if his or her state triggered "on" for EB in November 2008.

---

[30] Section 203(a)(2) of P.L. 91-373, as amended.

[31] Section 203(b) of P.L. 91-373, as amended

[32] The release schedule for LAUS data may be found at http://www.bls.gov/lau/lausched.htm.

[33] The benefit year is a one-year period during which a worker may receive benefits based on a previous period of unemployment. In all states, the beginning date of the benefit year depends on when a worker first files a valid claim, meaning the worker meets minimal wage and employment requirements.

Under the 2009 stimulus package (as amended), states have the option of ignoring the benefit year requirement and instead using EUC08 exhaustion as an eligibility requirement, as long as the state's EB period falls between enactment of the stimulus package and December 31, 2013. This has the effect of allowing more individuals to be eligible for the EB program.[34]

As described above, the EUC08 program contains a "reachback" clause under which EUC08 benefits were made available to individuals who had exhausted regular UC benefits with respect to a benefit year that expired during or after the week of May 6, 2007. Before the stimulus package, many individuals who had exhausted EUC08 benefits would have been ineligible for EB benefits if the state triggered "on" for EB after their benefit year expired. Under the stimulus package, however, all individuals who have exhausted EUC08 benefits would be eligible for EB benefits, regardless of the timing of their benefit years.

Methods for Determining 20 Weeks of Full-Time Insured Employment

States use one, two, or three different methods for determining an "equivalent" to 20 weeks of full-time insured employment. These methods are described in both law (Section 202(a)(5) of the EUCA) and regulation (20 CFR 615.4(b)). In practice, states that require any of these three methods for receipt of regular UC benefits *and* do not allow for exceptions to those requirements do not need to establish that the worker meets the 20 weeks of full-time insured employment. The three methods are listed below:

- earnings in the base period equal to at least 1.5 times the high-quarter wages; or

- earnings in the base period of at least 40 times the most recent weekly benefit amount, and if this alternative is adopted, it shall use the weekly benefit amount (including dependents' allowances) payable for a week of total unemployment (before any reduction because of earnings, pensions or other requirements) that applied to the most recent week of regular benefits; or

- earnings in the base period equal to at least 20 weeks of full-time insured employment, and if this alternative is adopted, the term "full-time" shall have the meaning provided by the state law.

The base period may be the regular base period or, if applicable in the state, the period may be the alternative base period or the extended base period if that determined the regular UC benefit.

The underlying reasoning behind the requirements seems to be the following:

- Because there are 13 weeks in a quarter, 1.5 times the high-quarter wage is roughly equivalent to 1.5 times 13 weeks of wages or about 20 weeks of wages. (Many states require high quarterly earnings of under $2,000, which works out to less than $4/hour under full-time assumptions. This is less than the federal minimum wage of $7.25/hour.)

---

[34] States would once again be responsible for 50% of the cost of new entrants to the EB program after December 31, 2013, however, as 100% federal financing of the EB plan ends. The federal government would continue to pay 100% of EB benefits for individuals who were receiving EB during the week ending on December 31, 2013 for the duration of their EB receipt.

- Similarly, because the weekly benefit amount is roughly equivalent to half the average weekly wage, 40 times the weekly benefit amount is roughly equivalent to 20 weeks of wages.

2009 Stimulus Provisions Affecting EB Financing

Under permanent law, EB benefits are funded half (50%) by the federal government through its account for that purpose in the UTF. States fund the other half (50%) through their state accounts in the UTF. The federal government pays 100% of EB *administrative* costs.

The 2009 stimulus package, as amended, temporarily changed the federal-state funding arrangement. The federal government finances 100% of EB benefits through December 31, 2013, through the EUCA of the UTF, with the exception of "non-sharable" benefits (generally, these are former state and local employees' EB benefits). The EB program's 100% federal financing has prompted some states to adopt the optional triggers to provide 20 weeks of extended benefits. The exception for non-sharable benefits, however, has made some states reluctant to adopt the optional 20-week EB triggers, or the stimulus provision that allows them to use EUC08 exhaustion rather than benefit year as a requirement for EB eligibility.

For individuals who are receiving EB payments on December 31, 2013, the federal government will continue to pay 100% of EB benefits for the duration of these individuals' benefits (but not for new entrants to the EB program starting after that date). The stimulus package also continued the temporary suspension of the waiting week requirement for federal funding until the week ending on or before June 30, 2014.[35]

Unemployment Insurance and the Sequester[36]

The sequester order required by the Budget Control Act of 2011 (P.L. 112-25) and implemented on March 1, 2013 (delayed by P.L. 112-240),[37] affected some, but not all, types of unemployment insurance expenditures:

- Exempt from sequester are UC, UCX, and UCFE payments.

- Subject to sequester are EB, EUC08, and most forms of administrative funding.

---

[35] States that do not require a one-week UC waiting period, or have an exception for any reason to the waiting period, pay 100% of the first week of EB. For information on state laws regarding this waiting week issue, see U.S. DOL's "Comparison of State Unemployment Laws, 2013," Chapter 3: Monetary Eligibility, Table 3.7, pp. 15-17 (available at http://www.workforcesecurity.doleta.gov/unemploy/pdf/uilawcompar/2013/monetary.pdf). P.L. 110-449 (as amended by P.L. 111-5, P.L. 111-118, P.L. 111-144, P.L. 111-157, P.L. 111-205, P.L. 111-312, P.L. 112-78, P.L. 112-96, and P.L. 112-240) suspends this requirement.

[36] For additional details on the sequester of certain components of the unemployment insurance system, see CRS Report R43133, *The Impact of Sequestration on Unemployment Insurance Benefits: Frequently Asked Questions*, by Katelin P. Isaacs and Julie M. Whittaker.

[37] For additional details on the sequester, see CRS Report R42050, *Budget "Sequestration" and Selected Program Exemptions and Special Rules*, coordinated by Karen Spar.

FY2013 Sequester of UI Benefits

The FY2013 sequestration percentage reductions applied to the budgetary resources provided for all of FY2013 (October 1, 2012, through September 30, 2013)—but the actual EB and EUC08 payment reductions began to be implemented the week beginning March 31, 2013. The Office of Management and Budget's sequester order for FY2013 required a 5.1% reduction to be applied on all nonexempt nondefense mandatory expenditures.[38] Thus, EUC08 and EB payments were required to be reduced by 10.7% for benefits paid for weeks of unemployment beginning on March 31, 2013, to meet the 5.1% reduction target for FY2013.

The U.S. DOL released guidance on how states should implement the FY2013 sequester reductions to unemployment benefits for FY2013.[39] These reductions generally began the week beginning on or after March 31, 2013. For states that were not able to implement these reductions by March 31, 2013, the amount of the benefit reduction increased.[40] No unemployment benefits already paid to individuals were recovered to satisfy the sequestration reductions.

FY2014 Sequester of UI Benefits

In FY2014, the Office of Management and Budget's sequester order requires a 7.2% reduction in all nonexempt nondefense mandatory expenditures.[41]

EUC08: FY2014 Sequestration

Consequently, the U.S. DOL has determined that EUC08 will be reduced by 7.2% for benefits paid for weeks of unemployment beginning on October 6, 2013, and ending December 28, 2013.[42] According to its guidance, the U.S. DOL will work with states individually to assist them in administering the FY2014 sequester of EUC08:

> Due to the extraordinary programming challenges states experienced during sequestration implementation for FY 2013, and the additional challenges presented by the further changes necessary for sequestration implementation for FY 2014, the Department has reached out to states with various options that may be used in order to achieve the required FY 2014 sequestration savings. Letters have been sent to each state approving the implementation

---

[38] Office of Management and Budget, *OMB Report to the Congress on the Joint Committee Sequestration for Fiscal Year 2013*, Washington, DC, March 1, 2013, http://www.whitehouse.gov/sites/default/files/omb/assets/legislative_reports/fy13ombjcsequestrationreport.pdf.

[39] Employment and Training Administration, U.S. Department of Labor, *Unemployment Insurance Program Letter (UIPL) 13-13*, March 8, 2013, http://wdr.doleta.gov/directives/attach/UIPL/UIPL_13_013_Acc.pdf.

[40] See pages 5 and 6 of UIPL 13-13, http://wdr.doleta.gov/directives/attach/UIPL/UIPL_13_013_Acc.pdf. Not all states implemented the sequestration reductions uniformly across all EUC08 beneficiaries. Several states were unable to implement the preferred method of reduction as outlined by the U.S. DOL and used alternative measures instead. For an overview of these alternative measures, see CRS Report R43133, *The Impact of Sequestration on Unemployment Insurance Benefits: Frequently Asked Questions*, by Katelin P. Isaacs and Julie M. Whittaker.

[41] Office of Management and Budget, *OMB Sequestration Preview Report to the President and Congress for Fiscal Year 2014 and OMB Report to the Congress on the Joint Committee Reductions for Fiscal Year 2014* (corrected version), Washington, DC, May 20, 2013, http://www.whitehouse.gov/sites/default/files/omb/assets/legislative_reports/fy14_preview_and_joint_committee_reductions_reports_05202013.pdf.

[42] Employment and Training Administration, U.S. Department of Labor, *Unemployment Insurance Program Letter (UIPL) 30-13*, September 27, 2013, http://wdr.doleta.gov/directives/attach/UIPL/UIPL_30_13.pdf.

---

strategy agreed upon by the Department and the states in advance of further specific guidance in this UIPL [Unemployment Insurance Program Letter.][43]

EB: FY2014 Sequestration

EB benefits will be reduced by 7.2% for any benefits paid for weeks of unemployment beginning on October 6, 2013, and ending September 27, 2014.[44] Only the federal share of EB benefit costs are subject to the sequester. The current 100% federal financing of EB benefits ends December 31, 2013. After December 31, 2013, when the federal share of EB benefit costs returns to 50% (and states finance 50% of EB benefits), states generally would be responsible for paying the amount of the EB benefit subject to sequester (i.e., making up the 7.2% reduction). However, under federal law, a state may reduce EB benefits by the amount sequestered if the state changes its state unemployment law and the reduction is equivalent to the sequester reduction.

---

[43] Ibid., p. 3.

[44] Ibid.

Appendix A. Unemployment Insurance Benefits

Figure A-1. Sequence of Unemployment Benefits: UC, EUC08, and EB

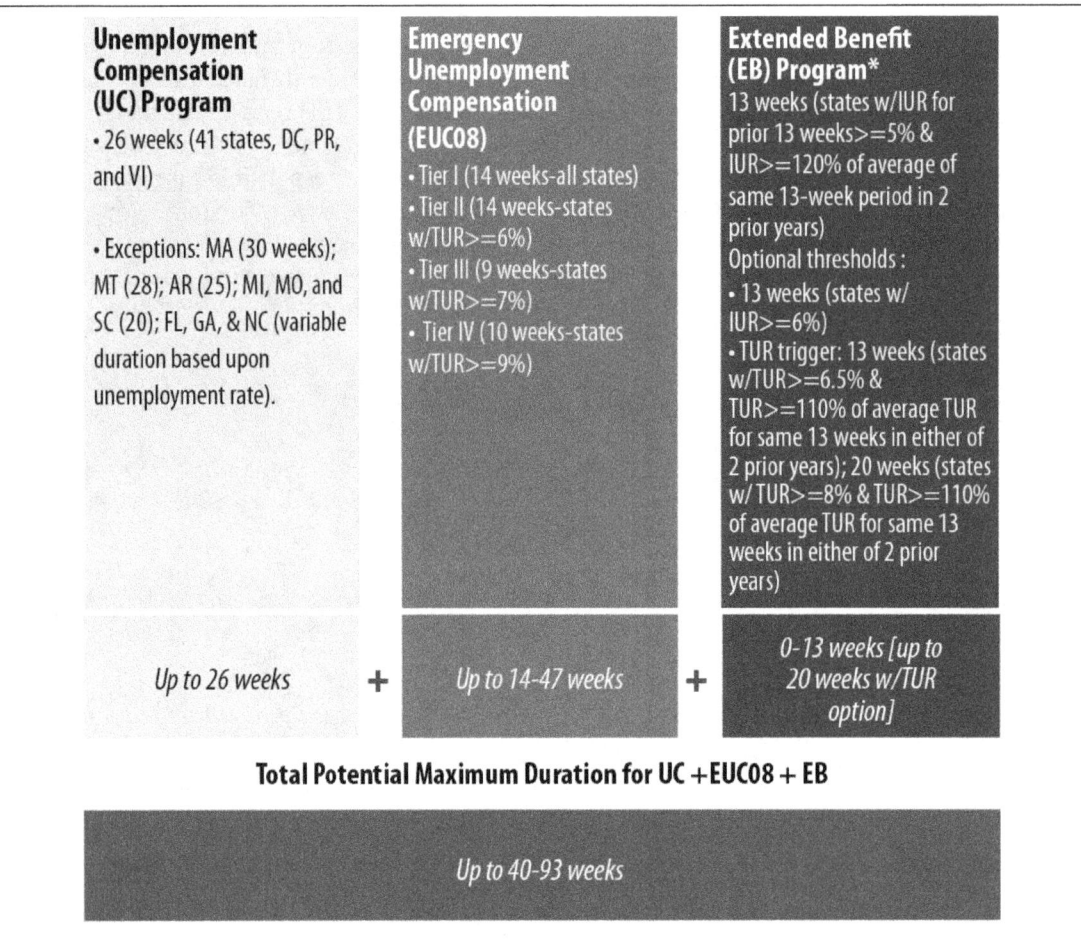

Unemployment Compensation (UC) Program
- 26 weeks (41 states, DC, PR, and VI)

- Exceptions: MA (30 weeks); MT (28); AR (25); MI, MO, and SC (20); FL, GA, & NC (variable duration based upon unemployment rate).

Up to 26 weeks

+

Emergency Unemployment Compensation (EUC08)
- Tier I (14 weeks-all states)
- Tier II (14 weeks-states w/TUR>=6%)
- Tier III (9 weeks-states w/TUR>=7%)
- Tier IV (10 weeks-states w/TUR>=9%)

Up to 14-47 weeks

+

Extended Benefit (EB) Program*
13 weeks (states w/IUR for prior 13 weeks>=5% & IUR>=120% of average of same 13-week period in 2 prior years)
Optional thresholds :
- 13 weeks (states w/ IUR>=6%)
- TUR trigger: 13 weeks (states w/TUR>=6.5% & TUR>=110% of average TUR for same 13 weeks in either of 2 prior years); 20 weeks (states w/TUR>=8% & TUR>=110% of average TUR for same 13 weeks in either of 2 prior years)

0-13 weeks [up to 20 weeks w/TUR option]

Total Potential Maximum Duration for UC +EUC08 + EB

Up to 40-93 weeks

*Under permanent law (P.L. 91-373 [26 U.S.C. 3304, note]), the EB program trigger lookbacks make use of unemployment rate data from either of the two previous years. Under temporary law (P.L. 111-312, as amended), however, states have the option to use the last three years of unemployment rate data for their EB program triggers. For the implications of providing fewer than 26 weeks of regular UC benefits on the calculation of EUC08 and EB maximum durations, see CRS Report R41859, *Unemployment Insurance: Consequences of Changes in State Unemployment Compensation Laws*, by Katelin P. Isaacs.

Source: Congressional Research Service.

Figure A-2. Benefits Available in Emergency Unemployment Compensation (EUC08) July 6, 2008-December 28, 2013

July 6, 2008 - Nov. 23, 2008	*Nov. 24, 2008 - Nov. 7, 2009*	*Nov. 8, 2009 - Feb. 18, 2012*	*Feb. 19, 2012 - May 26, 2012*	*May 27, 2012 - Sep. 1, 2012*	*Sep. 2, 2012 - Dec. 28, 2013*
13 wks –all states	**Tier I: 20 wks** –all states **Tier II: 13 wks** –if state TUR>6%	**Tier I: 20 wks** –all states **Tier II: 14 wks** –all states **Tier III: 13 wks** –if state TUR>=6% **Tier IV: 6 wks** –if state TUR>=8.5%	**Tier I: 20 wks** –all states **Tier II: 14 wks** –all states **Tier III: 13 wks** –if state TUR>=6% **Tier IV: 6 wks** –if state TUR>=8.5% (16 wks if no active EB & TUR>=8.5%)	**Tier I: 20 wks** –all states **Tier II: 14 wks** –if state TUR>=6% **Tier III: 13 wks** –if state TUR>=7% **Tier IV: 6 wks** –if state TUR>=9%	**Tier I: 14 wks** –all states **Tier II: 14 wks** –if state TUR>=6% **Tier III: 9 wks** –if state TUR>=7% **Tier IV: 10 wks** –if state TUR>=9%

Source: Congressional Research Service.

Notes: Because New York defines a week as a period from Monday through Sunday, the effective dates for New York are one day later than those shown above. For example, the EUC08 program first became active in all states except New York on July 6, 2008. The EUC08 program first became active in New York on July 7, 2008.

The total unemployment rate (TUR) is the 13-week average ratio of unemployed workers to all workers (employed and unemployed) in the labor market. The TUR is essentially a three-month average of the seasonally adjusted unemployment rate for each state published by the Bureau of Labor Statistics from its Local Area Unemployment Statistics (LAUS) data. It is possible to have tier III or tier IV available based upon a 13-week average insured unemployment rate (IUR). These options are not depicted in this figure. The IUR is a program-based statistic: the ratio of Unemployment Compensation (UC) claimants to individuals in UC-covered jobs. The ratio does not include those unemployed workers who are receiving EUC08 or EB payments, or any other type of unemployed worker except those who are currently receiving regular UC benefits.

For the implications of providing fewer than 26 weeks of regular UC benefits on the calculation of EUC08 maximum duration, see CRS Report R41859, *Unemployment Insurance: Consequences of Changes in State Unemployment Compensation Laws*, by Katelin P. Isaacs.

Appendix B. Summary of EUC08 Program

Table B-1. Emergency Unemployment Compensation Program:
Public Law, Benefits, Effective Dates, and Financing

Public Law	Benefit Tiers and Availability	Dates in Effect and Financing
Supplemental Appropriations Act of 2008, Title IV Emergency Unemployment Compensation (P.L. 110-252), signed June 30, 2008	13 weeks (all states)	7/6/2008-3/28/2009 (No benefits past 7/4/2009) Funded by federal Emergency Unemployment Compensation Account (EUCA) funds within Unemployment Trust Fund (UTF).
Unemployment Compensation Extension Act of 2008 (P.L. 110-449), signed November 21, 2008	Tier I: 20 weeks (all states) Tier II: 13 additional weeks (33 weeks total) if state total unemployment rate (TUR) is 6% or higher or insured unemployment rate (IUR) is 4% or higher.	11/23/2008-3/28/2009 (No benefits past 8/29/2009) Funded by federal EUCA funds within UTF.
American Recovery and Reinvestment Act of 2009 (P.L. 111-5), signed February 17, 2009	Same as above. [Act included several other interventions that augmented UC benefits: the Federal Additional Compensation (FAC) benefit of $25/week; at state option, EB benefit year could be calculated based upon exhausting EUC08 benefits; 100% federal financing of EB program; and the first $2,400 of unemployment benefits were excluded from income tax in 2009.]	2/22/2009-12/26/2009 (No benefits past 6/5/2010) Funded by general fund of the Treasury. (Additionally, the FAC program is funded by the general fund of the Treasury. The 100% financing of the EB program is funded by the EUCA funds within the UTF.)
Worker, Homeowner, and Business Assistance Act of 2009 (P.L. 111-92), signed November 6, 2009	Tier I: 20 weeks (all states) Tier II: 14 additional weeks (34 weeks total, all states) Tier III: 13 additional weeks if state TUR is 6% or higher or IUR is 4% or higher (47 weeks total) Tier IV: 6 additional weeks if state TUR is 8.5% or higher or IUR is 6% or higher (53 weeks total) [Act included 1.5 year extension of the Federal Unemployment Tax Act (FUTA) surtax.]	11/8/2009-12/26/2009 (No benefits past 6/5/2010) Funded by general fund of the Treasury. Extended FUTA surtax through June 2011. The estimated revenues collected from FUTA surtax provision were $2.578 billion and offset the estimated direct spending costs for unemployment insurance provisions of $2.42 billion.
Department of Defense Appropriations Act, 2010 (P.L. 111-118), signed December 19, 2009	Same as above.	12/27/2009-2/27/2010 (No benefits past 7/31/2010) Funded by general fund of the Treasury.

Public Law	Benefit Tiers and Availability	Dates in Effect and Financing
Temporary Extension Act of 2010 (P.L. 111-144), signed March 2, 2010	Same as above.	2/28/2010 (retroactive)—4/3/2010 (No benefits past 9/4/2010) Funded by general fund of the Treasury.
The Continuing Extension Act of 2010 (P.L. 111-157), signed April 15, 2010	Same as above.	4/4/2010 (retroactive)-5/29/2010 (No benefits past 11/6/ 2010) Funded by general fund of the Treasury.
The Unemployment Compensation Extension Act of 2010 (P.L. 111-205), signed July 22, 2010	Same as above. [Note this did not include an extension of the Federal Additional Compensation (FAC) benefit of $25/week for those receiving UC, EUC08, EB, Disaster Unemployment Assistance, or Trade Adjustment Assistance. The FAC expired on June 2, 2010.]	5/30/2010 (retroactive)-11/27/2010 (No benefits past 4/30/2011) Funded by general fund of the Treasury.
The Tax Relief, Unemployment Insurance Reauthorization, and Job Creation Act of 2010 (P.L. 111-312), signed December 17, 2010	Same as above.	11/28/2010 (retroactive)-12/31/2011 (No benefits past 6/9/2012) Funded by general fund of the Treasury.
The Temporary Payroll Tax Cut Continuation Act of 2011 (P.L. 112-78), signed December 23, 2011	Same as above.	1/1/2012-2/18/2012 (No benefits past 8/11/2012) Funded by general fund of the Treasury. P.L. 112-78 included offsets; for example, the auction of spectrum licenses and increased federal retirement contributions.
Middle Class Tax Relief and Job Creation Act of 2012 (P.L. 112-96), signed February 22, 2012	Tier I: 20 weeks (all states) Tier II: 14 additional weeks (34 weeks total, all states) Tier III: 13 additional weeks if state TUR is 6% or higher or IUR is 4% or higher (47 weeks total) Tier IV: 6 additional weeks if state TUR is 8.5% or higher or IUR is 6% or higher (53 weeks total); 16 weeks if no EB and all other conditions met (63 weeks total)	2/19/2012-5/26/2012 Funded by general fund of the Treasury.

Public Law	Benefit Tiers and Availability	Dates in Effect and Financing
Middle Class Tax Relief and Job Creation Act of 2012 (P.L. 112-96), signed February 22, 2012	Tier I: 20 weeks (all states) Tier II: 14 additional weeks if TUR is 6% or higher (34 weeks total, all states) Tier III: 13 additional weeks if state TUR is 7% or higher or IUR is 4% or higher (47 weeks total) Tier IV: 6 additional weeks if state TUR is 9.0% or higher or IUR is 6% or higher (53 weeks total)	5/27/2012-9/1/2012 Funded by general fund of the Treasury.
Middle Class Tax Relief and Job Creation Act of 2012 (P.L. 112-96), signed February 22, 2012	Tier I: 14 weeks (all states) Tier II: 14 additional weeks if TUR is 6% or higher (28 weeks total) Tier III: 9 additional weeks if state TUR is 7% or higher or IUR is 4% or higher (37 weeks total) Tier IV: 10 additional weeks if state TUR is 9.0% or higher or IUR is 6% (47 weeks total)	9/2/2012-12/29/2012 (No benefits past 12/29/2012) Funded by general fund of the Treasury.
American Taxpayer Relief Act of 2012 (P.L. 112-240), signed January 2, 2013	Same as above.	12/30/2012 (retroactive)-12/28/2013 Funded by general fund of the Treasury.

Source: Congressional Research Service.

Author Contact Information

Julie M. Whittaker
Specialist in Income Security
jwhittaker@crs.loc.gov, 7-2587

Katelin P. Isaacs
Analyst in Income Security
kisaacs@crs.loc.gov, 7-7355

www.ingramcontent.com/pod-product-compliance
Lightning Source LLC
Chambersburg PA
CBHW080748290526
45790CB00008B/3375